Healing

ILASIA PURNELL

Copyright © 2020 by Ilasia Purnell.
All rights reserved. No part of this book may be used or reproduced in any manner whatsoever without the express written permission of the publisher except for the use of brief quotations in a book review.

Printed in the United States of America

ISBN: 978-1-7334432-7-2 (paperback)
ISBN: 978-1-7334432-8-9 (ebook)

First printing, 2020
JayMedia Publishing
Laurel, MD 20708
www.publishing.jaymediagroup.net
Cover photo credit: @808dion (Instagram)

TABLE OF CONTENTS

INTRODUCTION 1

FATHER 3

BROTHER 5

EX 7

MOM 11

GRANDFATHER 13

GOOD FRIEND 15

SICK IN THE HEAD 17

ADVICE 19

AFFIRMATIONS WITH SCRIPTURES 21

SET FREE AND HEALING 25

Keep your head up no matter what you are going through.

INTRODUCTION

Loss. Skepticism. Depression... just to name a few.

I have gone through a lot within the relationships in my life. I need to express how these different relationships have shaped me.

But most importantly, I need to express how the most critical relationship of all, the one I have with God, has made the most significant impact in my life and has shaped who I am now as a woman.

I share them all with you. I had to get it out.

These are my stories.

I also share what I have learned through my life with advice and affirmations supported by biblical truths so that you can...

Be Free. Be Healed. In the precious name of Jesus

SMILE.

HEALING

FATHER

Hello world. At the age of 8 years old, I started to realize that my father was not really doing his part as a father. The only things I can remember are my father teaching me how to box and taking me to the basketball court. The year of 2011, my father lied to me about things changing. As the years have gone by nothing has changed as far as him doing his part as a father. The thing that really bothered me was when he used to leave me at my grandmother house, while he went to hang out with his girlfriend and her child. I always reached out my hand to my father by telling him how I felt but it seemed like he always pushed it away. Although this was the situation, I am now trying to build a relationship with him.

"Say to them that are of a fearful heart, Be strong, fear not: behold, your God will come with vengeance, even God with a recompence; he will come and save you."

Isaiah 35:4

BROTHER

Growing up with my older brother (we are two years apart), I went everywhere he went back when we were in elementary school because my mother was not around. He was responsible for me. So, after school, if he went to the store before going to aftercare, I went too. We used to walk to different fast food places together like the local carry out, McDonalds, Taco Bell etc. We use to have dogs. I did not like dogs and was terrified of them so I kept my room door closed all the time when I slept. Although my brother knew I was terrified, he would always open my door and let the dog come in my room. I would run out, close the door behind me, and run in my mother's room yelling and telling on him. When we were in elementary school, I used to have a crush on his friend that was of mixed races. I wrote in my diary about him. One day my brother invited him over when my mother was at work and he read my diary aloud to him. I do not know when he went in my room but when he read my diary aloud, I took it so quick, ran upstairs to my room, and closed the door because I was so

HEALING

embarrassed. We used to play fight and fight for real; he was just a typical big brother. He used to always make me laugh but there were times he made me mad by doing things to get on my nerves but that is how we became close. I used to look up to him until he started to get in trouble in school and with the law. Then he started to hang around the wrong crowd that did not have his best interest at heart. After he left me behind it really hurt my feelings. It seemed like he did not care anymore. He was so worried about the wrong things and it made me sad when he started to change. Due to the actions of my brother over the course of our relationship, it led me to stop looking up to him.

EX

When I was in ninth grade, I met a guy at school. We only said hi to each other the one time I saw him. Then after ninth grade, I did not go to that school any more. So back when Facebook was popping, I received a message in my dms from him. We were messaging each other for hours, and then he had to get off Facebook, so he asked for my number. I gave him my number and we talked every day on the phone. Then one day he wanted to meet up with me because he forgot what I looked like. After meeting up with me for the first time he asked to take me on a date, and we ended up going to the movies. I met his mom after the movies because she came to pick us up. Then she met my mother when she dropped me off at home. After that date, we were around each other all the time. I used to go to family functions with him, we went on trips together and we always used to be at each other's houses. I was fourteen going on fifteen and he was fourteen at the time, so we were young, but we always had fun together. After a while, there were some bumps in the

HEALING

relationship and tears. Once I started going to a new high school nothing felt right when it came down to us being around each other. During a situation we were dealing with at the time, he started asking questions like, "Why are you here with me? Why did you choose me?" Although we were not together anymore when prom came around, we were still going to go to together since we had been planning it for a long time. Our proms were on the same day, so I was going to go to his prom, but he decided to take some else. So, I was scrambling trying to find someone to take to my prom at the last minute. I really did not want to go anymore but my mother told me it was going to be a memorable moment that I did not want to miss. I truly hated prom because I had ended up taking my cousin and he did not make me feel better about prom. My friends did not do a good job of making me feel better about prom either. I cried at prom most of the night. I could not make it fun because all I thought about was what my ex did and wondered why he did it. It took a long time to get over the situation since it really hit me hard back then. I felt like I lost a big part of me because he was my best friend for so long while we were in the relationship. He was the only guy I ever dated, and we were both virgins while being together. He broke up with me without a reason and that was the icing on the cake for me. It put me in a fragile, broken state of mind because I was in love with him for years. I felt like he gave up on me and on us. This experience caused me to be afraid of losing anyone I truly cared about and as a result, it has caused me to be skeptical about dating again.

LOVE.

MOM

Growing up, my mother never gave me that much attention. She gave it mainly to my brother because he always got in trouble and to my little sister because she was the youngest. It did not bother me when I was in elementary or middle school because I did not know what depression or anxiety was back then. I was young and my focus was on school and having fun. During my childhood, I did not realize that there was not a mother-daughter bond between us. I did not realize that I was not getting the attention that wanted or needed until my 10th or 11th grade year and that is when I battled with depression. When I was in 10th grade, my mother stopped buying things for me and I was forced to get a job. I felt like while in 10th grade I should have just been focusing on going to school since that was the beginning of high school. I was not thinking about working when I was in 10th grade because I would get money from my grandparents every weekend I would go over there. After my brother moved out, my mom started to be hard on me and I never understood why. I have always been

HEALING

the one to not get in trouble in school or give her a hard time. At times, I felt embarrassed by her because she would yell at me or get on me for no reason in front of my friends. I say that because my friends would ask, "What did you do?" And I would say, "I do not know." As a middle child, there were times that I felt left out. My mom always came to my brother's rescue and she had to attend to my sister because she was a baby and needed the attention. It was not always like this. My mother and I used to make up dances together, I used to go to the studio with her when she used to record her songs, I was always around when she coached cheerleading, she used to do my hair, and we would have good talks when we would clean up. For these reasons, my relationship has gotten better. One day in particular I remember going to her broadcast and we talked about how I felt. Before then, she didn't know what was going on. As an adult, I prayed that our bond would get better and it did.

GRANDFATHER

When I was younger, I would go and do anything with and for my grandfather such as getting his newspaper and reading it with him, watching sports with him, going to the grocery store with him as well as helping him put the groceries away. I would be in the kitchen when he was cooking just to observe and keep him company. I would also go on all the trips with him. My grandfather was so supportive of anything I had done as far back as me graduating from elementary school. He would be there for every dance performance and also when I graduated. During the summertime after I graduated middle school, he went into the hospital. I would go to the hospital often and check on him. He did not let anyone know that he was sick prior to him being in the hospital. When I would go up to the hospital, he was not able to speak, so he wrote things down. I do not remember if he was in a coma which caused him to lose his speaking ability because before he was in the hospital, he was able to talk fine. I do remember this thing in his chest called a defibrillator which was a

HEALING

machine that helped him breath. The doctors had to unplug it and I don't know why but he was able to breath on his own for a while. I remember I would always want to go to the hospital store to get him things like cards and flowers. One card said *Get well soon Gran I love you* and it made him cry. I truly hated seeing him in that hospital bed and I thought he would come home real soon. I thought this every day for months. Then one day in 2010 my mother woke me up at 5:00 or 6:00 in the morning and told me my grandfather had died. I started crying immediately and I didn't want to be bothered all day. My mom had the nerve to ask me if I wanted to go to school. Why would I want to go to school on a day like this? This situation made me feel like I did not want to do anything or go anywhere.

HEALING

GOOD FRIEND

When I was in 9th grade, I had this good friend that I would be with every day after school. We used to go to the library to study and read books. We always walked to the rec center to play basketball, play games, and we would watch tv from time to time. We walked to get food sometimes and he even met my mom when she picked me up one day. He was the type of guy that I could talk to about anything and he would talk to me about things. A lot of people in the school knew how close we were. One day he did not come to school and after school I saw police, fire fighters and an ambulance in front of his house. I saw them because he lived across the street from the school. I did not know why they were there, and I did not think that something happened to him. It really did not click because it could have been anyone that lived with him. The next day I went to school, they asked for a moment of silence for him on the announcements. When they said his name, it did not hit me until they finished the announcement and one of my friends asked if I was okay. I cried all day because

HEALING

I felt like I lost someone I was really close with. Although he died before my grandfather did, I felt like I was just losing everyone I loved and truly cared for. I could not get over the fact that he killed himself because I was just with my friend the day before. I really wish there was something I could have done before this all happened. He was smart and goofy. He made me laugh every day and our bond grew unbreakable. He was nice to everyone; he had a good heart and spirit. He always kept a smile on my face no matter what he was going through. It felt like he was the only friend I had even though I had others. But I cherish every moment we had together.

HEALING

SICK IN THE HEAD

When I was in the 11th grade, a guy who was a friend to my brother would keep coming to my house knocking on my door. I would always tell him that my brother didn't live here anymore, and he would say that he knew that, he had come to see me and not my brother. I would ask him why he had come to see me, and he would say that he had always paid attention to me. One day, after he left, he found me on Instagram because I do not remember giving him my Instagram. He then messaged me and said, "Hi" and we talked for a little bit. Then he asked me to hang out with him, so I went to his house to meet him. I thought that we were going to go somewhere to sit or something. Instead we were in his house and he began touching me and I was telling him to stop and he kept touching me. Then he was trying to force me to kiss him I said, "No, I'm not kissing you." After that he began to unbuckle my belt to pull down my pants and I kept telling him to stop but he was still trying to pull my pants down. Then I yelled, "Stop! Get off of me!" really loud then he

HEALING

let go. He asked, "Why are you acting like I'm about to rape you? Because if I wanted to rape you, I would." I ran out of his house quick and I didn't look back. I did not care about how my clothes looked. I ran and did not look back. I even passed my house because I was scared that he would follow me to my house and force me to go inside. I did not tell anybody for a long time. I never thought that he would try to rape me. He was so careless or high or something of that sort because he was tripping. I do not know what made him try that.

ADVICE

Healing begins the moment you accept the hurt. It requires you to feel your emotions, recognize your ego that carries a story and accept that your soul has the capacity to prevail through it all. The healing process is not a quick process, but it will come, you must be patient. You must forgive yourself in order to realize which part of you still needs healing. I know that a lot of us in this world become bothered when people walk out of our lives, but when that happens that means that they were never attached to your destiny in the first place. Care about yourself and give yourself some self-love. You will start to feel better, love one another and help others to rise to the higher levels simply by pouring out love. Love is infectious and is the greatest healing energy. You will begin to heal when you let go of the past hurts, forgive those who have wronged you and learn to forgive yourself for your mistakes. Time heals all wounds of the past. Apologies, forgiveness and acceptance lightens the scars. If you don't heal what hurt you then you will bleed on people who did not cut you. Pray daily and stay focused.

HEALING

Get to know yourself by finding out what you like. That will be a big important part of the healing process. When you can tell the story and it does not bring up any pain, you know that you are healed. Do not look for healing from those who broke you. Healing at times needs an atmosphere of faith. Tell yourself you have courage even if you have to dig a little to find it. To increase your own healing ability set your intention for change with love.

AFFIRMATIONS WITH SCRIPTURES

"Behold, I will bring it health and healing; I will heal them and reveal to them the abundance of peace and truth."

(Jeremiah 33:6)

God loves me. Deeply and completely. The enemy loves it when I feel shame, condemnation, and self-loathing, but God's Word says I am precious in God's sight— accepted and valued.

(Isaiah 43:4)

God saw my abuse and did not condone it. Neither should I. I do not have to stay silent or bury the pain and trauma. The Lord hates all wickedness, including my abuser's sinful actions.

(Psalms 11:5)

I can pray for wisdom and entrust true justice to the righteous heart of God. He always has the last word—He brings justice to the unrepentant and great mercy to the repentant.

(Psalms 103:6)

I know I can forgive others because I have been so greatly forgiven. Bitterness will only make my pain worse and continue to wound others.

(Hebrews 12:15)

I can pray for my abuser's change of heart and repentance—that my abuser will seek the Lord, turn from wickedness, and learn to live a godly life so God will be glorified.

(Luke 6:28)

I do not have to live in fear like a victim. Peace and victory come as I study and rest in who I am in Christ.

(Ephesians 1:3–8)

As I run to the Lord who sees, heals, and comforts, I can use what the enemy meant for evil to bring glory and praise to God...

(Genesis 50:20)

HEALING

I can learn how to communicate clear, pure boundaries in all relationships and speak truth in love.

(Ephesians 4:15)

I must be aware of the enemy's schemes to control my responses and defeat me. I must saturate my life with Scripture and remember God's grace is greater than the condemnation I feel.

(1 John 3:20)

Knowing my thoughts will control my actions and responses, I must allow God to transform my thinking so I can make daily choices to please Him.

(Romans 12:2)

I will grow and heal as I rub shoulders with godly women who model how to respond with the pure love of Christ and trust the Lord to help me stand in dignity and strength.

(1 Peter 3:3–5)

HEALING

I can, as a member of the Body of Christ, be a part of holding abusers accountable—especially within the church.

(Matthew 18:15-17)

I can also encourage those who still struggle toward freedom from the pain and insecurities that arise out of sexual abuse.

(Galatians 6:2)

SET FREE AND HEALING

Second Peter 1:3 says, "His divine power has granted to us all things that pertain to life and godliness, through the knowledge of him who called us to his own glory and excellence." I've discovered everything I need to move forward in grace and strength comes from abiding in God's presence and the Word of God.

The path to thriving begins with God-focus, not self-focus. If we continue to gaze inward, we will always see our scars, but when we gaze on Jesus, we see His scars and remember He died to make us whole again. We can trust the One who loved us so completely.

I've grown in Christ, but it hasn't always been easy. I've had many questions, and my heart screamed for answers. Satan wants us to believe God is not good and does not care, but our Father God is never blind to the sins that hurt His people. He grieves over all sin and hates it. Sometimes the Lord deals directly with others' sinful behavior against us; other times, it's just not time yet. In mercy,

HEALING

God gives even the most evil among us opportunities to turn to Him and repent.

My great comfort is that Jesus understands abuse. He suffered great abuse and even death to give us life (see Isaiah 53). He brings hope for today, tomorrow, and most certainly, hope for dealing with hurtful past circumstances in victory.

I am free to love others sincerely and allow the Lord to work in my life and my abuser's life now that I have been set free from the bondage that chained me for so many years.

Although Jesus said He came to give me abundant life (John 10:10), sometimes I resort to survival mode when I allow myself to feel ashamed. In those moments, I forget who I am—or rather, whose I am. Jesus bore my shame on the cross; I don't need to bear it for one moment.

Though scars remain, God gives healing grace.

Father God, I ask You to bring victory and healing to those who suffer. Surround them with Your presence, help them see You as You really are, and show them the overcoming power in Your Word. Amen.

www.ingramcontent.com/pod-product-compliance
Lightning Source LLC
Chambersburg PA
CBHW021126080526
44587CB00010B/653